Hig
The SK
TOU

"The same spirit of playful mindfulness that Joseph Cornell has used to connect millions of children with the outdoors he now offers to us all. This book is a gift!" —Bill McKibben, founder 350.org, environmentalist

"*The Sky and Earth Touched Me* is an excellent guidebook for those who wish to live in harmony with nature. The wonderful exercises in this book—such as 'Expanding Circles' and 'Vibrant Peace Walk'—calm us, and help us feel oneness with the world around us."

> —Masahito Yoshida, Professor, World Heritage Studies, University of Tsukuba; Executive Director, Nature Conservation Society of Japan; Chairman, International Union for Conservation of Nature in Japan

"*The Sky and Earth Touched Me* offers a chance to experience nature's wonders deep within ourselves. Joseph Cornell's outdoor activities are a delight, showing both children and adults how to see and experience nature in ways they might not have thought possible. Imagine the lines of distinction between you and a tree or animal becoming blurred or disappearing altogether, as you realize you have become that tree or animal in a very real sense. Read the book and be inspired; do the activities and be transformed!"

> —Kathryn Gann, Director, Theosophical Society of America

"*The Sky and Earth Touched Me* is a phenomenal book. After reading it from cover to cover, I intend to absorb its every nuance over the coming months and years. Cornell's book is going to be a Nature-Bible-Workbook for us here at University of the Living Tree, which we will use for inspiration and as a reference tool for workshops and courses. Profound and movingly written, it is presented with clarity and simplicity."

> —Roderic Knowles, Founder of Living Tree Educational Foundation, Ireland, author of *Gospel of the Living Tree*

"Whether I have a few minutes or a few hours to spend in nature, the exercises in *The Sky and Earth Touched Me* enrich that time profoundly. I feel connected with and renewed by the beauty and power of the natural world. The lakeside meditation supported me through the last weeks of my father's life. During that challenging and precious time, I was easily able to access the memory and tranquility of the exercise." —Susan Sanford, naturalist and facilitator

"Joseph Cornell offers *The Sky and Earth Touched Me* as a generous gift for those wishing to re-awaken childlike curiosity and powers of nature observation within themselves and others. Practical, feasible activities, clearly explained, include vivid stories of wildlife and natural areas. Factual natural science lessons integrate fluidly with useful suggestions for nurturing emotional and aesthetic nature reverence, holistically encompassing the myriad ways humans connect with nature. Why not give it a try? Take a deep breath, slow down, calm your mind, and begin to reconnect with nature in the most fundamental way, honing skills basic both for ecologists and poets. The tips and techniques shared help participants achieve what sometimes takes weeks in a wilderness retreat, a sort of 'express train' to natural rejuvenation."

—Janet Carrier Ady, Senior Program and Policy Advisor, Division of Education Outreach, National Conservation Training Center, U.S. Fish and Wildlife Service

"In this time of increasing environmental and social unsustainability, *The Sky and Earth Touched Me* is an excellent resource to help people reconnect and relate deeply to nature, including other people, and through these experiences to love and care for creation. Through Cornell's wellness exercises that deepen peoples' psycho-spiritual relationships with nature will come new understandings and purposes for living that include healing, hope, and restoration in this time of increasing unsustainability of human civilization as we know it."

—James E. Crowfoot, PhD, Professor Emeritus of Natural Resources and Urban and Regional Planning, Dean Emeritus, School of Natural Resources and Environment, University of Michigan at Ann Arbor, MI; Former President of Antioch College, Yellow Springs, OH

"I have used Joseph's 'Flow Learning' techniques for years with meaningful results. Our students have touched Nature and have had Nature touch them. Their reflections have been deep, clear, and powerful. Joseph Cornell's newest book, *The Sky and Earth Touched Me*, opens a new door for us: He shows us how crucial close contact with nature is for healing one's body, mind, and spirit. The exercises in his book make the spirit reverberate with love for God's creation." —David Blanchette, Outdoor Education, Punahou School, Hawaii

"As a teacher, naturalist, and storyteller, I have used Joseph Cornell's Sharing Nature books as the core of much of my work. Now, with *The Sky and Earth Touched Me*, Joseph shows how to connect with nature on an even deeper level. I will use the techniques in this book in my own life, and share them with others—spreading them like ripples on a pond to create a more peaceful, kind, loving, and sustainable world. This book is an instruction manual for all who wish to live in harmony with Planet Earth."

—Frank Helling, U.S. National Park naturalist, storyteller, and educator

"Joseph Cornell does not merely inspire us to commune with nature, but engages us in experiential exercises that connect us with the natural world, not merely symbolically, but tangibly. Like John Muir, he teaches us how to have a personal relationship with flowers, trees, and wildlife. The sample exercises he offers are at once scientifically sound and spiritually enlivening. In an age where modern technology, industrial entertainment, and political stridency increasingly distract us, Cornell shows us how to pay attention to what it's really all about, and how to share that joy with others."

—Harold Wood, Coordinator, Sierra Club John Muir Education Team
& Webmaster, Sierra Club John Muir Exhibit—www.johnmuir.info

"With *The Sky and the Earth Touched Me*, Joseph Cornell sparks our consciousness through revelatory story and extraordinary exercises. Beautifully written, this book sums up the experience of raising one's awareness and connecting with all living things."

—Sandy Priya McDivitt, Co-Chair, Ananda College, Oregon

"Finally, a Sharing Nature book for adults! *The Sky and Earth Touched Me* gently guides us to cultivate a deep and very personal relationship with nature through wise words, scientific fact, and most importantly, direct experience. Joseph Cornell's inspired wellness exercises can't help but awaken within us a vital aliveness. The book is so full of light and love, that just reading it is uplifting, while putting it into practice is sure to transport you to a new level of awareness. I absolutely love this book and what it could do for our world!"

—Suzanne Ropiequet, Sacred Life Centre, wellness teacher and healer

"*The Sky and Earth Touched Me* will profoundly connect you to Nature in a way that you most likely have never previously experienced. Joseph Cornell not only shares his intimate knowledge of Nature with the reader, but shares how to connect with Nature in a uniquely experiential manner. This is not a book to read and put on the shelf—this is a book to experience. Whatever you do, take the time to step into Nature and enjoy the exercises that Joseph has designed to connect you to the joy and peace of Nature available to us all."

—Karl Sniady, President, The Coaches Training Institute

"I think we have all had, at least once, a magical experience in Nature. In the right mood, entranced by Nature's beguiling beauty, our attention became wholly immersed in the moment. But more often we bring our thoughts and worries into Nature with us, and though physically present, our minds are elsewhere. Cornell's book is full of simple practices that help us to lay aside our thoughts and worries and become truly present amidst the wonder—and recapture the soul-expanding magic of communing with Nature."

—Joseph Selbie, author of *The Yugas* and the Protectors Diaries series

"This book is a precious jewel. After having practiced medicine for over forty years, I will make a bold statement and say that our profession and those who come to us expecting to 'get well' would be well served were *The Sky and Earth Touched Me* required reading and study material in medical school.

"*The Sky and Earth Touched Me* shows us the way to open our hearts to all that surrounds us, and to remember, through experience, that we are part of a whole that will support, sustain, uplift, and expand our consciousness to that place of perfect wellness."

—Shanti Rubenstone, MD, Stanford University School of Medicine, 1983

"Throughout my career as a park ranger and environmental educator, I have integrated Joseph Cornell's *Sharing Nature with Children* activities and philosophy into my programs and lesson plans for K–12 students. In doing so, however, I discovered that 'sharing nature' isn't only for kids.

"*The Sky and the Earth Touched Me* invites you to personally experience the same joy of nature we are trying to instill in our youth. His new book speaks directly to the individual adult reader. With beautiful, soul-provoking quotations and photographs, interwoven with heartfelt, profound exercises, readers are prompted to experience nature's beauty, tranquility, and love.

"Whether you are a novice or an experienced naturalist, let this book be your companion while exploring nature. It will increasingly deepen your appreciation, relationship, and spirituality with the natural world."

—Roy Simpson, Education Specialist, Bureau of Land Management

"While practicing these outdoor exercises, I experienced deep mindfulness, peace, and a new connection to nature and myself. I immediately felt the transformative power and potential of this book for organizational and interpersonal growth. I will continue to lead and delight my business teams, networks, and family with Cornell's exercises."

—Adam Croan, Outdoor Products Industry Executive & Social Venture Leader

"Joseph Cornell offers accessible and simple techniques for remembering and reclaiming your JOY OF BEING. Practice these offerings with your friends and family and see if you can overcome the constant barrage of chatter in your own mind to become still, peaceful, and harmonious, with the love and enchantment available to all of us in nature if we are aware enough to pay attention.

I will be recommending this book to assist patients, family, and friends seeking to feel and experience the sacred joy of being, once again, or for the first time. True healing lies in gratitude, reverence, and communion with all that is; and if you have forgotten how to be in that consciousness, try an exercise or two in this book and experience it for yourself."

—Kristy Fassler, Naturopathic Doctor

"*The Sky and Earth Touched Me* is an extraordinary guide for healing this planet; just as Cornell has shared with us, we too can share the joy of nature with each other. As Gandhi and many great saints have told us, it is only in changing ourselves that we can change the world.

"This book will change the lives of many who journey to the heart of nature, and for those they touch. It is for anyone with the willingness to experience the healing power of the universe, bask in the light of the sun, and dance in the eternal joy of Life." —Zach Abbey, Natural Farmer

"In this book, Bharat has shared his deepest wellspring of joy, the source of the divine in nature. However you name that divine source, *The Sky and Earth Touched Me* will help you access it."

—Paul Green, teacher, Powhatan School

About Joseph Cornell's
NATURE AWARENESS BOOKS

"This man is connected to the heart of our planet, and the Earth's wisdom shines through him." —New Texas Magazine

"Reverence and respect for the nature life forces permeates Joseph Cornell's writings. He shares . . . ways to experience the joy and expansion of being one and at home with our Earth." —One Earth, Findhorn Foundation Magazine

"Joseph Cornell has a gift for sensitizing others to their natural world— and to their inner world." —Douglas Wood, author of *Grandad's Prayers of the Earth*

"This is absolutely the best awareness of nature book I've ever seen."

—Whole Earth Review

"Joseph Cornell is one of the most highly regarded nature educators in the world today." —Backpacker Magazine

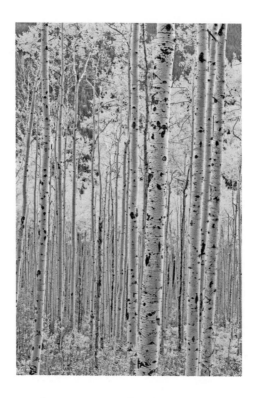

"I have grown taller from walking
with the trees."

—*Karle Wilson Baker*

The SKY *and* EARTH
TOUCHED ME

Sharing Nature® Wellness Exercises

JOSEPH BHARAT CORNELL

Crystal Clarity Publishers
Nevada City, California

ISBN: 978-1-56589-282-8
ePub ISBN: 978-1-56589-550-8

1 3 5 7 9 10 8 6 4 2

Cover and interior design by Tejindra Scott Tully

Library of Congress Cataloging-in-Publication Data

Cornell, Joseph Bharat.
  The sky and earth touched me : sharing nature wellness exercises / Joseph
    Bharat Cornell.
    pages cm
  Includes index.
    ISBN 978-1-56589-282-8 (trade paper : alk. paper) -- ISBN 978-1-
      56589-550-8 (epub)
  1. Nature--Psychological aspects. 2. Environmental psychology. I. Title.
  BF353.5.N37C668 2014
  155.9'1--dc23
                          2014001785

 www.crystalclarity.com
clarity@crystalclarity.com | 800-424-1055

~ CONTENTS ~

Part Two:

Part Three:

FOREWORD

I have had the privilege and good fortune to know Joseph Bharat Cornell for more than thirty years. Throughout those many years, he has brought extraordinary authenticity and grace to his work to bring peace and beauty to the world through direct experiences in nature.

We first met in the early 1980s when his landmark book, *Sharing Nature with Children*, was beginning to resonate with people throughout the world. It has now been translated into over twenty languages with a half-million copies in print.

Joseph's longstanding work and vision have nourished the roots of the emerging worldwide movement to reconnect children, families, and adults with nature. Joseph moves with a light step, warm laugh, and open heart to bring wonder, respect, and love of nature to learners throughout the world. I am among the many who are grateful for Joseph Cornell and his gentle, natural leadership.

Joseph founded Sharing Nature Worldwide in 1979 and has conducted workshops or given keynote presentations in more than thirty countries. Sharing Nature initiatives and organizations have formed in all regions of the world, including China, Indonesia, Japan, Korea, Europe, and North and South America. In Japan alone, thirty-five thousand Japanese adults have taken Sharing Nature's three-day training course for leaders.

While Joseph is perhaps most known for his best-selling *Sharing Nature with Children*, he is equally committed to sharing nature with people of all ages. This book, *The Sky and Earth Touched Me*, is a precious gift in that spirit. I am honored to write these words of thanks and celebration. Enjoy *The Sky and Earth Touched Me*, and share it with others you love. You will be among those contributing to a peaceful, healthy future for generations to come.

Cheryl Charles, PhD.,
Co-Founder, President and CEO Emerita
Children & Nature Network
Santa Fe, New Mexico
November 2013

by TAMARACK SONG

I have grown taller from walking with trees.
I have grown smaller from crawling with snails.
I have grown lighter from soaring with birds.
And along the way I have grown wiser
from forgetting what I think I know
and listening to teachers from forest and pond.
Every now and then when I go back to town
I forget that I need to speak English again.
For out in the woods it's a trill or a look
and I feel their feelings and dream their dreams
while everyone knows the yearnings I hold.
So I shed my fur and grab a pen
to tell what it's like to rise with the Sun,
to swim with a Turtle, to touch a Deer.
To enter their world and see through their eyes.
For these are the gifts I come to know
when the Sky and the Earth touch my soul.

We turn to nature for solace, inspiration, beauty, and mystery. We came from nature, and to nature we return. Yet how well do we truly know Her?

Many of us have become good technical naturalists. We have studied nature and can score well on a test, and some of us can successfully track an animal. Yet we struggle to come from the heart—we have little or no intuitive connection. We have lost a shade of what it is to be human.

This book is for those who don't want to wait until death to return to nature—who want to drink in her essence and feel in their marrow what it is like to be one with the mountains and waters and all living things. Here Joseph Bharat Cornell takes us on a deeply engaging guided journey to become a participant in the play of nature rather than a back-row observer.

This is not just another book on animal behavior or nature stories: Joseph gently helps us shed what separates us from nature. He then shows us how to embrace the soul of nature and let Her soul embrace us.

Rather than strolling through the woods, we become the woods. No longer will we have to be content with catching only occasional glimpses of animals—we will find that they are more relaxed around us, more willing to go about their normal lives while we watch. With each exercise, we feel less and less estranged from nature and more as though we've renewed an old and soul-satisfying relationship.

If you are new to nature immersion experiences, I encourage you not to skip around in the book, but to start with the exercises in Part One. With *Forest Bathing*, *Nature and Me*, and *Expanding Circles*, you'll learn to see with fresh eyes. You'll have undreamed-of experiences of being touched by the Sky and Earth.

Joseph states in the introduction to Part Two, "As we become inspired by nature's wildness and beauty, we naturally want others to also feel uplifted by nature." One of my favorite exercises is *Camera*—where two people become one, and one with nature, as they enter the silence and mentally photograph the affecting scenes before them.

Part Three brings it all home by showing us how silence connects us all, how to make our idealism practical, and how to live in oneness with nature here and now. As Joseph concludes, "The world didn't need changing—I needed changing." We discover the part of us that is a part of everything—the essence of us that is wise, precious, and beautiful.

~ ~ ~

Tamarack Song has been a student of the Old Way since his early youth. He is the author of *Entering the Mind of the Tracker* and *Song of Trusting the Heart*. Tamarack founded Teaching Drum Outdoor School, home of the Wilderness Guide Immersion Program, the only wilderness-living experience of its kind.

HOW *to* USE
THIS BOOK

Excursions to wild seashores and woodlands calm and refresh the human spirit. Recent scientific studies have shown that contact with nature increases the feeling of aliveness, awe, and connectedness, and reminds us of life's higher priorities. Even indoor natural environments can greatly influence us. Greening an office or classroom with plants has been proven to enhance cognitive functioning, creativity, comfort, and friendliness.

Affiliation with nature heals us and satisfies an essential human need.

Lakes, meadows, ferns, and butterflies are intrinsic to our well-being and wholeness. The powerful and rejuvenating exercises in this book can help you become immersed in nature's joyful presence and healing influence.

If possible, read *The Sky and Earth Touched Me* outdoors in a beautiful setting such as a garden, backyard porch, or nature park. The exercises can be practiced wherever there is a touch of nature.

As you do each of the exercises in Part One of the book, you will experience invaluable nature awareness principles. While Part One is primarily designed for personal inspiration, Part Two contains exercises that you can share with a friend or a group of friends.

~ PART ONE ~

The GREAT TEACHER *and* HEALER

rofound moments in nature can transform and shape our destiny. I can still vividly recall an experience I had as a five-year-old boy that awakened in me a lifelong fascination with marshes and migrating birds:

Playing alone outside on a cold foggy morning, I suddenly heard a startling chorus of "whouks" coming toward me through the air. I peered intently at the thick fog, hoping for at least a glimpse of the geese. Seconds passed; the tempo of their cries increased. They were going to fly directly overhead! I could hear their wings slapping just yards above me. All of a sudden, bursting through a gap in the fog, came a large flock of pearl-white snow geese. The sky seemed to have given birth to them. For five or six wonderful seconds their sleek and graceful forms were visible; then they merged once again into the fog. Seeing the snow geese thrilled me so deeply, that ever since then I have wanted to immerse myself in nature.

Nature's simplicity awakens in us a sense of serenity and belonging. While immersed in nature, many people feel a spiritual presence uniting them with the trees and surrounding hills. Of the silent wilderness of the Sierra Nevada mountains, John Muir proclaimed, "Here is calm so deep, grasses cease waving. . . . Wonderful how . . . everything in wild nature fits into us, as if truly part and parent of us. Our bodies . . . blend into the rest of nature, blind to the boundaries of individuals."

One moment of touching nature can inspire us for a lifetime. Mere exposure to nature, however, isn't always enough. One must not bring his restless thinking into the wilds, or the joy is lost.

I've spent most of my adult life helping others experience the natural world. To facilitate this experience, I've created many joyful and inspiring exercises that bring people face-to-face with nature.

In 1979 I published my first book, *Sharing Nature with Children*, which is now published in twenty languages and is used enthusiastically in every corner of the world. At the same time, I founded Sharing Nature Worldwide, an international nature awareness movement of leaders working with people of all ages.

Recently, Rita Mendonça, Brazil's Sharing Nature national coordinator, gave a training program in the Amazon for professional ecotourism guides, some of whom had worked in the area for forty years. Their attitude at first was that Rita (being from São Paulo) had little to teach them. But after participating in several experiential Sharing Nature activities, a woman approached Rita and said with deep emotion, "You are helping me find the forest inside of me! We don't know the forest in this way!"

The Sharing Nature wellness exercises fully engage us with nature. The exercises expand our sense of self by immersing us in the natural world and opening our hearts to all creation.

Because the exercises calm and internalize one's awareness of nature, people often experience remarkable results. Paul, who hikes the Appalachian or Pacific Crest Trail every summer, practiced the Sharing Nature wellness exercise, *I Am the Mountain*, for just four minutes. Afterwards he told me, "I was able to experience a state of heightened awareness that usually takes me a month in the wilderness to feel."

The HEART of NATURE

"My days in the wilderness will live with me always. Everything there is so alive and familiar. The very stones seem talkative and brotherly. One fancies a heart like our own must be beating in every crystal and cell. No wonder when we consider that we all have the same Father and Mother." —*John Muir: My Life with Nature**

ild creatures attract us because we have a natural affinity for those sharing the gift of life. Communing with fellow living beings helps us discover the richness of our own souls.

One evening at the Sacramento Wildlife Refuge in Northern California I observed five swans resting on a large pond. Because sundown was not far off, I stayed to see if the swans would fly off the water. Instead, hundreds of swans flew in from every direction and landed on the pond. As the sky turned violet over the Coast Range, flock after flock gracefully fell from the sky. Slowing their descent with outstretched wings, the swans seemed suspended in midair as they drifted downward. Long after the sun had set and the scene had disappeared in total blackness, I continued to hear the splashing and "*woo-ho, woo-ho*" of arriving flocks.

* Excerpts from Joseph Cornell, *John Muir: My Life with Nature* (Nevada City: Dawn Publications, 2000).

During magical encounters with nature, one is like a cell fed by osmosis—absorbing the immediate environment. During osmosis a cell not only receives from its environment but gives something of itself in return. In the case of human beings, we give back joy of communion and gratitude. As Meister Eckhart said, "What a man takes in by contemplation . . . he pours out in love."

The pioneering Japanese environmentalist, Tanaka Shozo, said, "The care of rivers is not a question of rivers but of the human heart." Through love, we begin to feel ourselves connected to everything around us. Our actions toward other beings become more caring, because we understand that, in harming another, we are harming a part of ourself.

To create a society that truly loves and reveres the natural world, we must offer its citizens life-changing experiences in nature. One moment of entering deeply into nature can inspire in people new attitudes and priorities in life.

A friend of mine as a child was so enchanted by the stars that she'd stare for hours into the night sky. She told me, "I couldn't understand why people weren't all outside gazing up at the sky in wonderment. Didn't they see the stars?" For children, the world is magical because everything is alive.

In his book *The Hidden Heart of the Cosmos*, Brian Swimme writes, "The Indians of South America teach that to become human 'one must make room in oneself for the immensities of the universe.'"[*]

Imagine yourself gazing at a mountain lake that's particularly stunning. When you are deeply attentive, everything becomes alive and vibrant. Then, suddenly, worries about the past or future steal your attention away from the present moment. As

[*] Brian Swimme, *The Hidden Heart of the Cosmos* (Maryknoll, NY: Orbis Books, 1996).

soon as your mind wanders, your connection with the aliveness and beauty of your surroundings vanishes. To merge with the sea of life, empty the mind of distractions, so that the great sea can race in and fill you.

In the following pages, you will find innovative exercises that will help you experience a joyous connection with the natural world.

FOREST BATHING

"I hear the wind among the trees
playing celestial symphonies."
—*Henry Wadsworth Longfellow*

When we walk through a forest, nature's benevolence flows into us as sunshine flows into trees. Beneath soaring pines and giant, spreading oaks, one's thoughts naturally become expansive and harmonious.

Forest Bathing, or *Shinrin-yoku*, is the Japanese practice of going to the forest to receive mental and physical healing. I first learned about Forest Bathing years ago in the Japanese Alps.

Forest plants emit essential wood oils and airborne chemicals to protect themselves from insects and decay. Studies show that forest aromas benefit humans as well. Researchers have discovered that "forest bathing" reduces stress, lowers blood sugar, increases concentration, strengthens the immune system, builds up vitality, and even has anti-cancer benefits.

All cultures recognize that trees uplift the human spirit. To ancient people, trees were channels for the gods; forests were humankind's first temples and sanctuaries.

Trees, living high in the sky, receive 95 percent of their sustenance from the atmosphere. Drawing nourishment from the sun and sky, trees express a divine benevolence. Buddhist scriptures speak of the unlimited kindness of trees: how they give generously, and offer protection and shelter to all beings.

Begin your walk in the forest by finding a magical portal between two trees. Pass through the doorway, keeping your senses alert.

* Feel the presence of the trees around you,
* Follow their trunks high into the sky,
* Observe their spreading branches.
* Listen to the voices of the birds, and of the trees.
* See and feel the wind flowing through the forest.
* Smell and breathe in the healing woodland fragrances.

RECIPROCAL BREATHING

Gaze into the sky...and locate the sun. Observe the surrounding trees absorbing the sun's light energy, making plant sugar, and discharging oxygen through photosynthesis.

An average-sized tree releases enough oxygen each day to sustain four people. Breathe deeply; fill your lungs with life-giving oxygen, given to you by your forest friends. As you exhale, gratefully return the favor, offering carbon dioxide to the nearby trees.

On the underside of a leaf are the largest number of tiny openings (stomata) through which air enters and exits a tree. Reach out and gently hold a leaf, bringing your nose close to the leaf's underside. Inhale the oxygen released by the tree and then exhale carbon dioxide into the leaf. As you breathe in and out, be aware of how interconnected you are with the forest, and of the reciprocal relationship all beings have with one another.

> "Between a human and a tree is the breath.
> We are each other's air." (*Margaret Bates*)

Continue walking and feel yourself united with all that is. Use the words of George Washington Carver to open your heart to all creation:

> "All flowers talk to me and so do hundreds of little things in the woods. I learn what I know by watching and loving everything."

BECOME PART OF THE FOREST

If you could live in this forest by becoming a tree, what kind of tree would you choose?

Find a good place to stand—and face the sun.

Close your eyes. Feel yourself rooted firmly in the earth—and living high in the sky. Feel the rays of the sun warming you. Bathe in the sunlight and open air.

Visualize your body as a leaf. Feel the sun's rays flowing into you, turning light into life. A large, healthy oak may have 250,000 leaves. Extend your arms and imagine you are all the leaves on a tree—each leaf receiving the light of the sun.

Listen to the sounds of the forest—close by—and far away.

Open your eyes. See the many varied expressions of forest life surrounding you: the trees—bushes—birds—rocks—grasses and flowers.

All these things live with you in cooperation and harmony. Delight in the benevolence and unity all Life shares.

~ ~ ~

FIND A BEAUTIFUL PLACE in the forest and reflect on the following thought:

"All terrestrial things are essentially celestial."
—*John Muir*

This insight is especially true for trees. In what ways do trees and forests inspire you? What noble qualities do you feel trees express?

A few words ABOUT FOREST BATHING

All plants have phytoncides: active substances with antimicrobial properties that kill or inhibit the growth of bacteria, microscopic fungi, and protozoa. Some trees release into the atmosphere volatile phytoncides that are capable of producing an effect at a distance. Studies have shown that the air in coniferous forests, and particularly in young pine forests, is practically sterile and free of harmful microflora.

In 1982 the director of the Japanese Forest Agency hypothesized that "bathing" in a phytoncide-rich environment would promote better health.

He proposed the idea of forest bathing for relaxing the mind and for stress management.

In 2004 the Japanese Ministry of Agriculture, Forestry and Fisheries initiated scientific studies to prove the therapeutic effects forests have on human health. Their studies showed positive results for numerous areas of physical health.

In Japan today there are forty-two approved Forestry Therapy Bases offering mental and physical healing. At some sites, forest therapy patients stay for two nights; they receive a medical checkup on arrival, spend their free time walking in the woods, and have another checkup before leaving. Patients are able to see significant improvements on their final exam. Many Japanese companies include forest therapy in their employee healthcare benefits and wellness programs.

To receive the greatest benefit from their time in the forest, people are encouraged to stimulate and use all their senses.

For more information about Forest Bathing, contact the International Society of Nature and Forest Medicine at the following address: www.infom.org/resources.

NATURE *and* ME

he first time I tried the *Nature and Me* exercise was in Bidwell Park in Northern California. My wife and I sat alongside an exquisite canyon stream lined by a lush forest. Mayflies danced above flowing water; large leaves fluttered with every breeze; sounds of falling water sang throughout the canyon. This simple activity helped us become dynamically aware of the presence of life around us.

After playing *Nature and Me*, while our minds remained calm and our senses alert, we began walking along a streamside trail. Suddenly, in the shallow creek, we saw rocketing underwater two brown, grayish forms: river otters!

Blending perfectly with the river rocks, the otters were difficult to see. For ten minutes we observed them frolicking and swimming. During this time, forty people walked by; none of them saw the otters. We would have missed them, too, if we hadn't practiced *Nature and Me*.

Psychologists have discovered that people have hundreds of self-talk thoughts every minute. The *Nature and Me* activity helps quiet restless thinking so that we can be open to life's beauty.

"With an eye made quiet by the power
of harmony, and the deep power of joy,
we see into the life of things."

—*William Wordsworth*

Find a captivating spot outdoors, such as a flower-filled meadow or a forest glade. Sit down (or remain standing) and rest both hands, palms down, lightly on the thighs.

During this exercise you're going to observe natural phenomena that capture your attention: for example, the texture of a tree's bark, a field of flowers waving in the wind, or a bird calling deep in the forest. Don't think about what you notice; just let your awareness flow from one observation to another.

Each time you see something, gently press a fingertip on your thigh to note the observation. Counting this way helps keep your concentration fully focused on your observation. Touching the leg also helps you feel that everything you see is part of you.

Use the ten fingertips on your hands to count your observations in batches of ten. Start with the tip of your left hand's little finger and count across to your right hand, ending with its little finger. Go across as many times as you like. Two to three times (twenty to thirty observations) works well.

Another way to play *Nature and Me* is to focus on one object, such as a tree or a boulder, that has many interesting features. With each observation, you will discover more and more detail about your subject: perhaps you will notice its silhouette or shape, its color and texture, its immediate environment. The suggested number of observations for this version is fifteen to twenty. Children and adults who are more scientifically inclined usually prefer this second version of *Nature and Me*. After finishing this exercise, players enjoy sharing their discoveries in small groups.

 *Children* may count their observations too quickly, thinking that the goal is to see how *many* observations they can count. Be sure to tell them that the point of *Nature and Me* is to *see* and *experience* nature really well. Prepare children for the activity by sitting with them and sharing aloud two or three observations.

The SKY and EARTH TOUCHED ME

Prairie grasses swaying in the wind—clouds drifting in the sky—songbirds flocking in a nearby tree—all make the heart sing. In her book *Touch the Earth*, T. C. McLuhan tells of an Inuit woman shaman celebrating the joy of being *moved and carried away* by the sea and weather:

> The great sea
> Has sent me adrift,
> It moves me
> As the weed in a great river.

We aren't merely observers of natural beauty. Everything we observe in nature is a part of us, because our soul contains the whole world. People enjoy being in nature because there they see ennobling qualities they want for themselves. In its myriad forms, nature helps enrich and expand us.

Richard Jefferies, the nineteenth century English writer and naturalist, spoke of everything in nature—a flower, a lake—as "touching him and giving him something of itself." He "spoke to the sea . . . and desired its strength." He addressed the sun, and consciously drew upon the soul equivalent of its light. He looked at the sky, gazed into its depths, and felt the "blue sky drawing his soul toward it, and there it rested."*

* Richard Jefferies, *The Story of My Heart*, 1883.

The way to *feel* nature inside you is to internalize your awareness. You can do this by first centering yourself, then relating from your center to the center of whatever it is that you're observing. For example, if you're watching a river, feel inside you the movement of its flowing water. The more you can do so, the more you'll feel nature as part of you.

‹—⟆ *To practice* ⟆—›
THE SKY AND EARTH
TOUCHED ME

Go to a beautiful natural area that feels vibrantly alive, such as a small stream lined with maple trees, a flowery mountain meadow, or an aspen forest. (One can also do this exercise indoors by looking out a window.)

1. When something captivates you, relate to it from your center to its center. Touch its essence and feel it becoming alive in you.

2. Feel that aspect of nature awakening equivalent soul qualities inside you. For example, a towering mountain may inspire feelings of higher aspiration.

3. Look lovingly at what has captivated you, and mentally include its name in the following sentence:

> *The* _____ *touched me*
> *and gave me part of itself.*

For example, if you observe a raven soaring high in the sky, say, "The raven touched me and gave me part of itself."

Continue to practice as you sit or walk, saying, "The _____ touched me," or, if you prefer, "The Creator touched me."

~ ~ ~

Many people, John Muir said, are like little marbles, rigidly alone, "having no conscious sympathy or relationship to anything." We are surrounded by other people and nature's beauties to help us expand our consciousness and self-identity. The more you commune with the living essence of nature, the more you'll feel the joy of the universe passing through you.

EXPANDING CIRCLES

> "Man is not himself only, . . .
> He is all that he sees;
> all that flows to him from
> a thousand sources."
>
> —*Mary Austin*

A teacher in the Southwest once asked the children in his class to draw pictures of themselves. He recalled, "The American children completely covered the paper with drawings of their bodies, but my Navajo students drew themselves differently. They made their bodies much smaller and included in the picture the nearby mountains, canyon walls, and dry desert washes. To the Navajo, the environment is as much a part of who they are as are their own arms and legs."

The understanding that we are a part of something larger than ourselves is Nature's greatest gift. With this understanding, our sense of identity expands and, by extension, so does our compassion for all things. *Expanding Circles* is a wonderful practice for overcoming egocentricity and enlarging one's sense of self.

David Blanchette is a teacher at the Punahou School on Oahu Island, Hawaii, where every year he leads thirteen-year-old students on a nature walk along a remote and wild coastline. Below are comments two of his students made after practicing *Expanding Circles*:

> I felt euphoria. I felt like I was one with everything around me.

> I was a calm ocean wave gently rolling towards the shore. I was the reef, feeling the cool water roll over me. Every part of me was moving and flowing in harmony.

Everyone enjoys gazing out across large lakes, fields and rolling hills, and other expansive landscapes. *Expanding Circles* greatly enhances your "gazing," by helping you focus more clearly on what you're seeing. After practicing this exercise in the mountains, a woman said, "At first I felt as though I were composing a picture; then suddenly I found I had stepped into the picture."

Practicing *Expanding Circles* helps one consciously affirm, and intuitively sense, his oneness with the natural world. When I do this exercise, I experience the great, harmonious sea of life of which I am a part.

To practice
EXPANDING CIRCLES

Because one's mind is drawn to movement, look for a place that has natural movement of some kind—such as a rippling lake or swaying trees. *Expanding Circles* works best if you sit where you have a panoramic view, and also an interesting foreground. For example, sit where there are flowers and grasses and perhaps a shrub close by, trees a little farther away, and a hill or mountain ridge in the distance.

- Sit down, close your eyes, and become aware of your body. Listen to the sounds of life around you—far away—and nearby.

- Open your eyes and extend your awareness just a few feet beyond your body to the nearby grasses, pebbles, and insects. *Try to feel that you are in everything you see as much as you are in your own body.* Feel yourself moving in and becoming alive in the natural world around you.

- Practice for a minute or so. Whenever your mind wanders, gently bring it back to what is before you.

- Extend your awareness farther to include the nearby shrubs and trees—twenty—thirty feet away.

- Relax and allow your attention to flow spontaneously, from the closest grasses and pebbles to the nearest trees. Feel that everything you see is part of you.

- Continue expanding your visual awareness in gradual stages—to fifty yards—a hundred yards—to the distant ridges—and into the vast blue sky.

- All the while, keep the awareness of yourself in what is closest to you, as well as all the way out to the distant mountains and sky. Let your awareness flow freely—naturally—to whatever interests you. *Feel inside yourself*—the sky—trees—and waving grasses.

Practice *Expanding Circles* for as long as you feel inspired. I have used this exercise for several hours at a time in such places as the Grand Canyon. There I've observed the changing play of light and shadow—and ravens soaring and diving in the sky. For your first time, I recommend trying the exercise for 10–15 minutes.

LIVING *in*
the PRESENT

t was late spring, and snow still covered the Sierra Nevada high country. While hiking back to my car, I went down the wrong side of a ridge and into unfamiliar territory.

When I realized my mistake, there wasn't enough daylight left to retrace my steps. Because I didn't have a coat, it was imperative that I get to lower elevation and warmer, snow-free ground. I knew that continuing my present course would eventually bring me to a road—if not that night, certainly by morning.

Fortunately, when in my early twenties, I had already learned in dramatic fashion the importance of staying centered in myself. In Death Valley, friends and I were staying with the chief naturalist at the national park. I went for a long walk late one afternoon, going much farther than I intended. I realized that I couldn't make it home before dark.

I wasn't afraid, but because I was embarrassed that people might have to look for me, I began to jog back.

Twinkling lights soon appeared from the park staff's residences; I was still miles away. Then the night enveloped me, making it impossible to see my immediate surroundings. I had traveled cross-country, so there wasn't a trail to follow. I continued to run toward the far distant lights.

Suddenly, the sandy, pebbly soil gave way to hard rock. I immediately stopped; solid rock, I knew, might mean a cliff ahead.

Peering into the darkness, I inched forward and tossed a rock in front of me. It took the stone too long to hit the ground: a rocky precipice was just ahead.

I realized how close I had come to disaster and was glad that I'd been paying attention. After feeling and searching with my feet, I found a steep ravine and carefully made my way down the thirty-foot-high cliff face.

After descending the rocky precipice—and breathing a sigh of relief—I had a revelation: I couldn't afford to worry about inconveniencing others. I needed to concentrate completely on my current surroundings and situation. Once I became clear about my priorities, the rest of the trip was uneventful.

Now, while descending the unknown ridge in the Sierra Nevada, I drew on my previous experience in Death Valley and felt completely relaxed. I realized that I might have some challenges ahead and might be bivouacking for the night. Knowing that fear and imagination often cause unwise decisions, I was determined to remain anchored in the serene timelessness of the natural world. As I did so, I found my walk becoming more and more joyful, even though the daylight was nearly gone and the outcome uncertain.

Well after sundown I reached a large lake and began walking along its shore. When it was almost dark, I saw in the distance two men fishing from a boat. I wanted to ask them where I was, but because yelling such a long way would disturb my inner peace, I kept on walking, feeling the vibrant, aliveness of the present moment, which was the only thing that seemed important.

When I came to a small cove, I saw another fisherman on the far bank. Now I was able to ask him in a calm, normal voice the name of the lake. "Spaulding," he replied, as he and his fishermen friends walked away. I was familiar with this lake; I now knew where I was.

Minutes later, as I cautiously made my way in the dark, I heard one of the fishermen ask, "Why don't you know the name of the lake?" To his direct question, I calmly explained how I had come to the lake by mistake. The man exclaimed, "But your car is eleven miles away, and it's nighttime! We'll drive you there."

My fisherman's friends disagreed with this plan, and I couldn't blame them. But I was feeling so free and blissful inside that I didn't want the night to end. I sat in the backseat of their car, comfortably letting things unfold, as they discussed quite energetically whether to drive me or not. I felt perfectly fine with whatever they decided.

My friend and advocate eventually convinced his friends to drive me to my car. While driving my own car home that night, I felt deeply grateful for the experience of joyous freedom that comes with living in the present.

The more you completely accept the present, the more energy you'll have to enjoy the present. Being present connects you with the joy that permeates all Life. When you're calm and centered, outer events seem always to work out for the best.

The VIBRANT PEACE WALK

eel the joy, serenity, and love that come from being fully aware of the present moment. John Muir said that to know trees (and all of nature) we must be as free of cares and of a sense of time as the trees themselves. When we quiet our internal dialogue and are no longer self-preoccupied—every leaf, flower, and rock will speak to us.

The secret to experiencing nature is to still our thoughts so that we can fully receive and merge with the world around us. Li Po, the Chinese poet, beautifully expresses how a mind that is still becomes mirror-like:

> The birds have vanished in the sky,
> and the last cloud drains away.
> We sit together, the mountain and I,
> until only the mountain remains.

The senses become heightened when we live in the present. Every tree, birdsong, and cloud is vivid and joyous because our attention is totally focused in the here and now.

We see the world as being not separate, but unified with us, and we feel great delight as we sail with the clouds and soar with the cranes high across the sky.

Thoreau's Advice:
Henry David Thoreau was serious about his walks in nature and gave the following advice for anyone contemplating taking a walk outdoors:

> We should go forth . . . in the spirit of undying adventure, never to return. . . . If you are ready to leave father and mother . . . wife and child and friends, and never see them again—if you have paid your debts, and made your will, and settled all your affairs, and are a free man—then you are ready for a walk.

"When in the wilds, we must not carry our problems with us or the joy is lost." —*Sigurd Olson*

CALM YOURSELF

The breath reflects one's mental state. As the breath becomes calmer, so does the mind, and vice versa.

As you sit or stand quietly for a few minutes, observe the natural flow of your breath. Do not control the breath in any way. Simply follow it with your attention. Each time you inhale, think "still." Each time you exhale, think "ness."

Repeating "still—ness" with each complete breath cycle helps focus the mind and prevents your attention from wandering from the present moment.

During the pauses after inhaling and exhaling, stay in the present moment, calmly observing whatever is in front of you. If thoughts of the past or future disturb your mind, calmly bring your attention back to what is before you, and continue repeating "still—ness" with your breathing.

BECOME EVERYTHING

"Let my mind become silent,
And my thoughts come to rest.
I want to be
All that is before me.
In self-forgetfulness,
I become everything."

—*Joseph Cornell*

When your mind wanders, repeat the above poem. Doing so will help bring you back into the present.

FEEL YOURSELF IN EVERY SOUND AND MOVEMENT

As you walk, feel that everything around you is a part of you. Feel yourself in the trees, standing tall and firm. Feel inside of you the movement of their branches and leaves as they sway and flutter with the slightest breezes.

Become the birds as they flit from branch to branch. Listen to their calls and feel their sounds resonating within you.

Follow the wind by the sounds and movements it creates as it flows through, around and over trees, meadows, and hills.

Feel yourself in every sound, movement, and creation of Nature.

"[It's w]onderful how everything in wild
nature fits into us . . . .
The sun shines not on us but in us.
The rivers flow not past, but through us."

—*John Muir*

LIVE EXPANSIVELY

If your mind begins to dwell on the past or to anticipate the future, focus your thoughts with the following practice:

~ As you walk ~
Make a smile with your whole body
and joyfully repeat these words:
I am peace—I am joy.
I am in all things.

Always live expansively. Enjoy the contrast between being self-absorbed and small—and embracing a larger world.

~ ~ ~

RESOURCES: *Listening to Nature* and *John Muir: My Life with Nature*, both by Joseph Bharat Cornell.

I AM
the MOUNTAIN

hen we are silent and still, the walls that separate us from nature vanish. J. Allen Boone, the author of *The Language of Silence*, made this profound observation:

> Whenever an Indian and I met for the first time, an invisible ceremony always took place.

The Native American would stand motionless and would silently "read" Boone's heart to discover the kind of man he was. Boone said this inner listening and rapport was the secret to the Native American ability to converse with animals.

The *I Am the Mountain* exercise connects your heart with the hearts of all nature. In this simple yet profound meditation, players internalize their awareness by looking for something in nature that attracts their eye, then feeling its living essence *inside* their own heart. When one relates to life from his heart (or center), he's in touch with the spiritual essence of Life itself, within himself and all nature.

Zach, a workshop participant, remarked, "The *I Am the Mountain* exercise took me to places I wasn't capable of going on my own. Yesterday I sat by the lake for a couple of hours and didn't have nearly the experience I had today while playing the exercise with my partner for four minutes."

◦⊱ *To practice* ⊰◦
I AM THE MOUNTAIN

I Am the Mountain can be practiced with another person or alone. To begin, look for a quiet outdoor place that is entrancing.

Choose someone to be the "prompter," and someone to be the "responder." The prompter sits or stands behind the responder to allow him an unobstructed view.

The prompter begins by quietly repeating the words "I Am." After each time the prompter says "I Am," the responder looks for something in nature that captivates him—perhaps a cloud sailing across the sky or the wind playing music in the forest. Whatever it is, the responder *feels* its living reality inside himself. He enjoys this feeling for a few moments, then quietly says a simple word or phrase that describes his experience of what he's observing. For example, the exchange may unfold in this way:

(Prompter) "I Am"—
(Responder) "the drifting cloud."

"I Am"—
"the waving branches."

"I Am"—
"the exhilaration of the wind racing across the lake."

After a while, the prompter can substitute phrases such as "I Love" or "I Receive" for "I Am,"

as in these examples: "I Love"—
"the serenity I feel;" "I Love"—
"the blue flowers"; "I Receive"—"a
wonderful joy in my heart."

The prompter and the responder
can continue the phrase and response exchange for about five
minutes. Switch roles as you feel to.

After players have played both roles
(prompter and responder), they
can relax and enjoy the serenity of
nature within and all around them.

Having one partner repeat "I Am" (or "I Love,"—"I Receive,"
etc.) keeps the responder focused and in the present moment.
Practicing *I Am the Mountain* with a friend creates a shared
sense of communion with nature and with each other.

Once you've experienced the benefits of this exercise with another person, you can practice it on your own during outdoor
excursions. Regularly practicing *I Am the Mountain* increases
your receptivity to, and communion with, the natural world.

The BENEVOLENCE
of LIFE

n 1887 Sir Francis Younghusband, then a young British military officer, was asked by his superiors to travel from Beijing, China to India by way of the Gobi desert and the Himalayan Mountains.

Younghusband was the first European to successfully cross the world's largest desert and highest mountain range. Since he did not share a common language with his guides, he spent day after day essentially alone in the silent wilderness. He describes this daring journey in his book, *The Heart of Nature*:

"To enable my eight camels to feed by daylight, I used to start at five o' clock in the afternoon and march till one or two in the morning. . . . The sunset glow would fade away. Star after star would spring into sight till the whole vault of heaven was glistening with diamond points of light. Above me and all round me stars were shining out of the deep sapphire sky . . . And a great stillness would be over all . . .

"In this unbroken stillness and with the eye free to rove all round with nothing in any direction to stay its vision, and being as I was many weeks' distance from any settled human habitation, I often had the feeling of being more connected with the starry firmament than with this Earth. . . .

"I knew also that the number of stars, besides those few thousands which I saw, had to be numbered in hundreds of millions. All this was astonishing, and the knowledge of it filled me with wonder at the immensity of the Starry Universe. But it was not the mere magnitude of this world that impressed me. What stirred me was the Presence, subtly felt, of some mighty all-pervading Influence which ordered the courses of the heavenly hosts and permeated every particle.

"We cannot watch the sun go down day after day, and after it has set see the stars appear, rise to the meridian and disappear below the opposite horizon in regular procession, without being impressed by the order which prevails. We feel that the whole is kept together in punctual fashion, and is not mere chaos and chance. The presence of some Power upholding, sustaining, and directing the whole is deeply impressed on us. And in this Presence so steadfast, so calm, so constant, we feel soothed and steadied. . . . Deep peace and satisfaction fill our souls."

Below, Younghusband tells about a later visit to Tibet:

"After arrival in camp I went off into the mountains alone. It was a heavenly evening. The sun was flooding the mountain slopes with slanting light. Calm and deep peace lay over the valley below me . . . I seemed in tune with all the world and all the world seemed in tune with me. . . .

"After the high tension of the last fifteen months, I was free to let my soul relax. So I let it open itself out without restraint. And in its sensitive state it was receptive of the finest impressions and quickly responsive to every call. I seemed to be truly in harmony with the Heart of Nature. . . .

"And my experience was this . . . I had a curious sense of being literally in love with the world. . . . I felt as if I could hardly contain myself for the love which was bursting within me. It seemed to me as if the world itself were nothing but love. . . .

"[M]y experience was no unique experience. It was an experience the like of which has come to many men and women in every land in all ages. It may not be common; but it is not unusual."

HARMONY RUNS THROUGH ALL LIFE

Once, while camping in the Cascade Mountains, I entered a small subalpine valley filled with shallow, bubbling streams and wildflowers. The feeling of bliss in the valley was so palpable, so thrilling, that when it was time to leave I had to drag myself away.

John Muir continuously experienced a joyous, benign presence in wild nature. He disagreed with advocates of Darwin's evolutionary theory who emphasized only nature's strife and competitiveness. He would also disagree with the sentiment expressed by a present-day scientist: "When we look at nature, we are only looking at the survivors."

Far from such a "survival of the fittest" view, forest ecologists have discovered that plants don't behave as individuals competing with one another. Trees are united with other trees through their root system underground and share nutrients depending on which tree most needs them. In one experiment researchers draped shaded cloth completely over one tree so that it couldn't produce food from sunlight. The scientists discovered that through a spidery network of mycelia, or living fungi cells, nearby trees gave the shaded tree the nutrients it needed.

The nineteenth-century Russian scientist, Peter Kropotkin, eagerly sought in eastern Siberia proof of evolution's "survival of the fittest" premise. To his surprise, the young scientist discovered that the most successful animals weren't the most competitive ones, but those who coped with the harsh environment primarily through cooperative behavior. Applying his Siberian experience to humans, Kropotkin asked rhetorically, "Who is the fittest: those who are continually at war with one another, or those who support one another?"

Nearly every traditional society operates on the basis of highly cooperative relationships; in most traditional cultures over-competiveness is viewed as a sign of insanity.

Once a class of Navajo children taught their Anglo-American teacher a valuable lesson in human relations. During the teacher's first week at their school, he asked one of the Navajo students to answer a simple question. The young boy couldn't answer correctly, so the teacher asked if anyone else knew the answer. The other Navajo children stared straight ahead and wouldn't respond.

Because he felt that most of the students knew the answer, the teacher was puzzled by their silence. Later, the teacher learned why no one had raised his hand: the young Navajos didn't want their classmate to lose face. Their friend's well-being and self-confidence were far more important to them than impressing the teacher.

THE WORLD IS NOT
THE SAME TO ALL PEOPLE

There is a fable about two traveling dogs, Tom and Buddy, who visited a small town. Tom, finding the front door of a building open, boldly walked in for a look. To his surprise, he saw a hundred snarling dogs. Frightened, Tom fled the building.

A little later, Buddy, unaware of what had happened to his friend, discovered the same door and happily went inside. To Buddy's delight, he saw a hundred smiling dogs, all wagging their tails. As Buddy left the building, he said to himself, "The dogs in this town are such nice canines, I think I'd like to live here."

Why was Buddy's experience so different from Tom's? The answer is that the room was filled with a hundred mirrors, and each dog saw his own reflection one hundred times. Tom, mistrusting the other dogs, snarled to defend himself, while Buddy, expecting the other dogs to be friendly, happily greeted them and thus received a hundred friendly greetings in return.

Like the mirrors in the story, the world reflects our thoughts and expectations back to us.

If we honor the sacredness of life in all beings, we will perceive harmony everywhere. "A beautiful soul dwells always in a beautiful world." (Ralph Waldo Emerson)

CALMNESS REVEALS
THE BENEVOLENCE OF LIFE

Sir Francis Younghusband's exalted experiences in the Gobi Desert and Tibet were born out of his countless days in the silent wilderness. The stillness, he said, "was so profound that, when at the end of many weeks I arrived at a patch of grass and trees, the twittering of the birds and the whirr of insects sounded like the roar of a London street."

The purity of nature brings out the purity in us. Birds, stones, and flowering trees don't have egoic awareness. The lack of ego-affirmation in nature is the reason we feel peaceful in wild places.

Mankind is the only species that has strong ego-awareness; this self-focus separates and isolates him from the rest of creation. The problems in the world today have their roots in this aspect of human nature.

Communion with nature comes in stillness, which quiets selfish emotions and attitudes. We can actively cultivate inner calmness through the practice of meditation. In Chapter Ten, you'll learn how meditation enhances receptivity to nature and reveals life's intrinsic goodness.

Before doing this exercise go to a beautiful forest (or visualize a forest in your mind):

Lift your face to feel the sun's warmth. For four and a half billion years the sun's gravity has held us in place—at the perfect distance—to safely send its light and warmth. Feel the sun's rays bringing life to the forest.

Gaze at the nearby trees. See how they reach into the sky. Eighty percent of a tree's mass lives in the atmosphere. A tree's substance comes not from the earth, but from the sky, where it turns air and light into life.*

Observe the trunk, branches, and leaves of a larger tree. Where does the mass of the tree come from? The answer is—carbon, which comes from the carbon dioxide in the air.

Only one percent of a tree is alive. A tree grows outward from its trunk and skyward from the tips of its branches. The deadwood, comprising ninety-nine percent of its body, provides the foundation for the tree to climb ever higher in the sky.

Like the sun, trees are a benign influence in this world. Forests are the lungs of the earth and provide food and shelter for countless creatures. Their shade and transpiring water moder-

* Around 95 percent of a tree's substance (carbon) comes in the air. The other five percent comes from nutrient-bearing water from the soil. Trees acquire carbon from the CO_2 in the air through the process of photosynthesis and release back in the air O_2 and a little H_2O.

ate the temperature and make life easier for other forest inhabitants.

Scientific studies show that trees calm us and provide spiritual and creative inspiration. In city neighborhoods trees create a sense of place and encourage people to be friendlier and have more positive interactions.

Trees also heal; people recover from surgery more quickly if they can see trees through their window.

> "(A tree has) unlimited kindness and benevolence
> that makes no demand for its sustenance and
> extends generously the products of its life activity;
> it affords protection to all beings." (*Buddha*)

The sun and trees are beautiful symbols for the benevolent presence that pervades creation. Harmony is the unifying principle of life; when we cooperate with the flow of life, we unite with the stream of love that animates all beings.

To deepen your sacred bond with trees, and with all life, go to a favorite forest grove and repeat the following words from Melissa Krige's *Trees of Light Meditation*:

> As the forests exhale
> so we inhale.
> And as we exhale
> so the forests inhale.
> In giving we receive
> and in receiving we give.

As you inhale and exhale, feel yourself giving and receiving breath and life from the nearby trees and other forest inhabitants.

ALL GOOD THINGS
COME *from* STILLNESS

he Buddhist monk, Godo Nakanishi, once spent several days sitting quietly on a snow-covered mountain. The birds living there noticed him, but fear of humans kept them a safe distance away. As the monk continued to meditate, he became more and more absorbed in the inner silence. Gradually, because of the wonderful peace Godo emanated, the wild birds lost their fear and accepted his presence. A few birds, apparently attracted to the serene monk, landed and perched on his motionless body.

The greater one's calmness, the greater the harmony one feels with his environment. As you read the following visualization, notice how calmness intensifies perception. Read each paragraph, then close your eyes and see its imagery in your mind:

- Imagine your mind as a pristine lake—encircled by mountains. See how the lake's surface reflects its surrounding environment—the mountains, trees, and sky.

- Now picture your thoughts as restless winds that ripple the lake's surface. These winds prevent you from seeing a clear reflection of the mountains.

- As your thoughts slow down and the breezes cease— once again you see the image of the mountains reflected perfectly in the lake of your mind.

When the lake was disturbed by restless winds, it couldn't reflect the mountains clearly. When the lake became calm, however, mountains, rocks, trees, and sky were perfectly mirrored on the lake's surface. So too does the human mind, when perfectly calm, flawlessly reflect one's higher reality.

THE WANDERING MIND

Unfortunately, the human mind is seldom quiet. Psychologists have said that people generate about three hundred self-talk thoughts a minute. Two Harvard researchers, Matthew A. Killingsworth and Daniel T. Gilbert, in 2010 discovered that 47 percent of the time adults think about something other than what they're doing.*

I once demonstrated this phenomenon to a group of twenty-five educators in Canberra, Australia. I asked each one to focus on a beautiful tree as long as he was able to, and to raise his hand when his attention wandered from the tree to other thoughts. After six seconds every hand was raised. The educators were amazed to see how restless their minds were.

When the mind wanders away from the present moment, one cannot expect to feel the deep rapport he desires with other people or with nature.

COMMUNE WITH LIFE

The birds landed on the Buddhist monk not because they found his body a convenient place to perch, but because they were attracted to his aura of peace. Interestingly, this monk later founded Japan's Wild Bird Society for the protection of native birds.

* Matthew A. Killingsworth and Daniel T. Gilbert, *Science* 330 (November 12, 2010).

As one quiets his uniquely human desires and restlessness, animals feel a growing sense of kinship. Barriers raised for self-preservation disappear and true communion becomes possible.

While meditating outdoors, many times animals have approached me trustingly. On one occasion I became aware of a large male deer sitting quietly in front of me. Later, during my meditation, I began to visualize and bless the deer. Immediately, the deer stood up, came over and for twenty minutes gazed intently at me from two feet away. Early on he sniffed once, just to let me know he was standing there.

Wilderness travelers often report having moments of great exaltation and joyousness. In my early twenties, while backpacking in the wilderness of Yosemite National Park, one evening I experienced a feeling of profound stillness. I felt my consciousness of self expanding to include the nearby glacial lake and surrounding mountains. The experience was so thrilling and joyful that I longed to have the same state of awareness all the time. I knew I couldn't live permanently in the wilderness. Instead I sought the inner wilderness: I learned to meditate and began a daily practice of cultivating a sense of oneness with life wherever I was.

LEARN AND PRACTICE MEDITATION

The benefits of meditation are numerous: inner peace, an expansion of self-identity, harmony with and love for others, creativity, vitality, and intuitive wisdom. Meditation will also help you gain more from the exercises in this book.

You can cultivate inner peace by practicing the following simple yet profound meditation technique. People from many different religious traditions use this meditation practice with tremendous success.

To practice
WATCHING THE BREATH MEDITATION

Preparation:

One of the best ways to relax the body is first to tense it. Then, as you relax, you will find a release of tensions you didn't even know existed. Begin your meditation experience by practicing the following two relaxation techniques. The first exercise relaxes your body, and the second calms your mind.

1. Inhale and tense the whole body, then throw the breath out and relax. Repeat this exercise three times to help rid your body of unconscious tensions.

2. The breath reflects one's mental state. As the breath becomes calmer, so does the mind, and vice versa. Before you meditate, relax by doing this simple breathing exercise:

Inhale slowly counting one to four, hold your breath to the same count, then exhale to an equal count. This breath cycle is one round of "even-count breathing."

You may either increase or decrease the number of counts as you find comfortable, but keep the length of inhalation, retention, and exhalation equal. Practice "even-count breathing" six times.

Meditation: As the breath becomes calmer and more refined during meditation, you may experience a joyous feeling of peace. Practice the following meditation technique to help calm your breath, your mind, and your whole being:

Inhale deeply, then slowly exhale. Wait for the breath to come in of its own accord, and watch its inflow. As the breath flows out naturally, again observe the movement. Don't inhale and exhale deliberately, but instead simply be an observer.

Notice and feel the movement of breath on the inside of your nose, with your attention on the breath itself, not on the nose.

Be particularly aware of the rest points between breaths. Enjoy the peace, and the feeling of inward release and freedom that you feel when your body is without breath.

Practice for ten minutes if you can. When you finish observing your breath, continue to sit quietly and enjoy the stillness and serenity you feel.

❀

Learn more about meditation by visiting *The Gift of Inner Peace* website: *www.giftofpeace.org*. To find out more about the Watching the Breath Meditation, click *Try Meditation* and follow the links. I created this website to introduce people to the joys and benefits of meditation.

A saint once asked his disciple to meditate whenever he saw an expanse of water so that he would be reminded of the vastness of his soul. To practice the *A Lake Is Like the Mind* exercise, find a tranquil pool of water in a stream or pond. The pool should ideally be small enough to give you a feeling of intimacy and serenity.

The pool of water should be at least eight inches deep. Collect six stones each about the size of a duck's egg. If the pool is tiny, gather proportionally smaller stones.

A lake's surface—like the human mind—is always changing. Sometimes the lake is calm and serene; other times a breeze, falling leaf, or splashing fish might ruffle its surface. In every case, the lake's placidity is disturbed by something external to itself. The mind is strengthened by meditation so that passing phenomena don't disturb it, just as the lake's deeper water remains unruffled no matter what happens on its surface.

To begin the exercise, find a comfortable place to sit that overlooks the water. Place your six stones beside you and gaze at the water, letting its placidity calm you. Do your best to stay in the present moment.

Every time you notice you've become distracted and are no longer grounded in the here and now, cast a stone in the water. Carefully observe each stone's splash and the ensuing ripples spreading outward—how the water (representing your mind) is disturbed and no longer mirror-like. Note the impact inattentive thoughts have on one's awareness.

It is normal to have thoughts during meditation. The trick is to let the thoughts pass by without seizing and embellishing them. When the stone's ripples start to dissipate, feel yourself letting go of all thoughts, and delight in the joyful serenity that comes with living in the present.

Keep gazing at the water until you have thrown all the stones.

Peace and awareness require stillness of mind, just as the surface of a lake must be completely calm to perfectly reflect the sky. Only in stillness can you discover the hidden depths of your spiritual nature.

GIVING *to* LIFE

hose who perceive Nature's underlying harmony and benevolence have tremendous impact on others. John Muir has been one of the most effective voices for conservation the world has ever known. His effectiveness sprang from his experience of life's "joyous inseparable unity." When Muir spoke of his encounters with wild animals, trees, and mountain storms, his listeners felt they were actually there. Few have brought nature to life as Muir did. His great love for all living things gave him a rare understanding of the natural world.

Muir's writings and enthusiasm were the chief forces that inspired the conservation movement. Robert Underwood Johnson, a leading conservationist of Muir's day, said of John Muir's seminal influence: "All other torches were lighted from his."

I attended college during the Vietnam War, and, like many young people, I opposed the conflict. Because of my deep desire for world peace, I majored in International Relations at Chico State University. I soon realized, however, that the prevailing self-interest of people and nations would continue to make world peace unattainable.

One day, while sitting on a bench overlooking Bidwell Creek on campus, I felt an overwhelming sense of joy and calmness. The sky and the nearby trees were vivid and pristine. A feeling of deep peace stayed with me for hours. "This is the real peace," I thought. I realized I could share this experience by helping others connect deeply with nature. I designed a "special major" that I called Nature Awareness, and began my lifelong quest to discover ways to commune with nature.

Your consciousness determines how you relate to life. If, for example, your spirits are uplifted and inspired, your thoughts naturally become altruistic. On the other hand, if your energy is low and depressed, you're likely to be self-absorbed and negative. If you try only to explain things to people (without uplifting their consciousness), your hope for a change in their behavior is likely to fail, because people usually think and act according to their present level of awareness. But if you uplift people's consciousness, you can truly change their attitudes and behavior.

The heart understands new and deeper truths. If you want to motivate people, first touch their hearts, because their hearts' feelings will inspire their thoughts and behavior.

The deepest feeling of all is *calm* feeling. Emotional feeling reacts to life from a personal viewpoint. Calm feeling is receptive; it is like a mirror that receives and reflects life clearly.

SERVE THE WORLD
WITH EQUANIMITY

As one becomes sensitive to life, it is natural to feel the suffering of others. One may also feel discouraged—powerless to help humanity overcome destructive, and self-destructive, tendencies. But few would think of reacting as extremely as my friend Ursula.

In the 1990s, I received a desperate letter from Ursula, who introduced herself as a twenty-seven-year-old German environmentalist and educator. Ursula, who cared deeply for nature, was outraged over the ongoing ruin of the earth. For many years she'd worked to change people's behavior, but had finally given up. She felt the only option left was direct action: "I believe my struggle will lead me to prison or death! All I need is people with weapons." She then requested the address of an anarchist group in the United States.

I wrote Ursula to offer her a positive perspective. Years passed without a word in reply, and I often wondered what had become of her. After five years, I finally received a reply: "I had just finished scouting a car manufacturing plant and choosing the places to plant the explosives when your letter arrived. If I hadn't received it, I'd be in prison today. I've carried your letter with me for these five years and frequently discussed its contents with my anarchist friends, many of whom agreed with its positive message."

Here are the principles for positive change that inspired Ursula to rethink her strategy:

When you let other people's behavior affect your inner peace, you give your power away. Sooner or later you're going to be disappointed by the actions of others. Will you then let their behavior stop you from doing what you feel inspired to do?

People have become disillusioned when the world doesn't agree with them. The only person you have control over, ultimately, is *you*. Your real responsibility is to change yourself. You first need to be what you want others to become. "Always Shozo was watching others and not himself; and because he did not look into himself, he had no true understanding of others." (Tanaka Shozo)

To stay positive, energetic, and loving, it's important to be inner-directed and act from your own center of inspiration. A journalist once asked Mother Teresa of Calcutta, "Don't you feel your efforts are hopeless? You can help only a small fraction of the people that need care." Mother Teresa replied, "God has not called me to be successful; He has called me to be faithful." Because Mother Teresa was so beautifully faithful to her own principles, thousands emulated her.

The key to personal sanity (and to avoiding burnout) is to work energetically for your ideals, while focusing not on the results but on the quality of your service. You can control only what you put out, not what you receive. If success in your undertakings depends on acceptance by others, success is really out of your hands. People who remain non-attached have greater endurance and love, because their enthusiasm burns steadily and isn't extinguished by external events.

For decades, Gandhi and many others sought their country's independence from British rule. A newspaper reporter, seeing Gandhi working fifteen hours a day, seven days a week, once asked him, "Do you ever take a vacation?" Gandhi smiled blissfully and replied, "I'm always on vacation." Gandhi always acted from within himself; although there were many struggles and disappointments, his inner inspiration continuously empowered and sustained him.

When life's nobler qualities inspire your actions, those actions are highly attractive to others. Keeping your inspiration immediate and flowing is essential; otherwise, your efforts are no more effective than ironing with an unplugged steam iron.

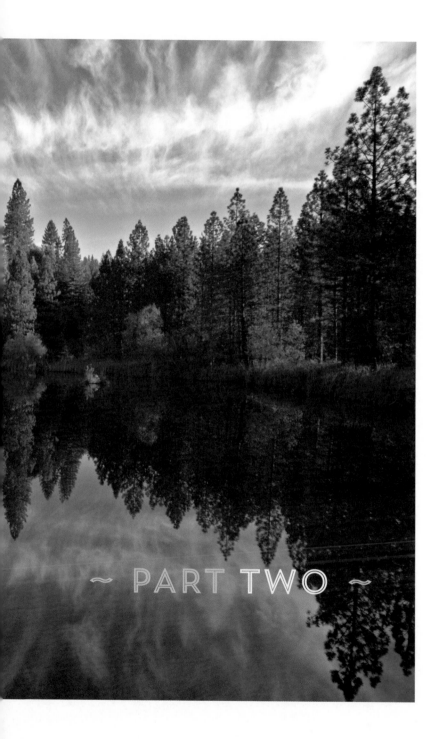

~ PART TWO ~

SHARING
with FRIENDS

As we become inspired by nature's wildness and beauty, we naturally want others to also feel uplifted by nature. To share *The Sky and Earth Touched Me* exercises with others—to see loved ones totally absorbed as they saunter serenely through the forest—is deeply rewarding for the leader.

The Sky and Earth Touched Me exercises are easy to facilitate. People all over the world are successfully sharing these activities, and—with a little thought and practice—you can too. Take the time to experience the exercises yourself before leading them. You will find that you can introduce them with confidence and conviction. For your first sharing, I recommend inviting friends who would be especially appreciative of the activities.

Exercises like *Forest Bathing*, *The Vibrant Peace Walk*, *Watching the Breath*, *Camera*, and *The Trail of Beauty* (the last two are featured in this section) are excellent activities to begin a nature immersion session.

Below is a way to sequence the exercises to immediately engage people and guide them to deeper contact with nature. Feel free to experiment and create your own sequences.

Sharing Nature Sequence

* Camera

* I Am the Mountain

* Forest Bathing

* Vertical Poem

* Watching the Breath
  or Nature and Me)

* The Trail of Beauty
  (*or* The Sky and Earth Touched Me)

* The Birds of the Air

To further enhance your outdoor adventures, you can add exercises from my book, *Sharing Nature: Nature Awareness Activities for All Ages*. If you're leading a group larger than a few friends, you'll want to read in this book the section describing *Flow Learning*™, a highly effective outdoor learning strategy that gently, almost magically, guides others to uplifting nature experiences.

CAMERA

amera is one of the most powerful and memorable exercises in this book. In a simple way, it quiets distracting thoughts and restlessness so that one can see clearly.

Camera is played with two people: one person is the photographer and the other the camera. The photographer guides the camera—eyes closed—on a search for beautiful and captivating pictures. When the photographer sees something he likes, he points the camera at it, framing the object he wants to shoot.

The photographer signals the camera to open his eyes (the lens) by tapping twice on the camera's shoulder. A third tap three seconds later tells the camera to close his eyes again. For the first picture, it may help to say "Open" with the first two taps, and "Close" with the third.

It's important that the camera keep his eyes closed between pictures, so that the three-second "exposure" has the impact of surprise. Encourage photographer and camera to remain silent (speaking only if absolutely necessary) to enhance the camera's experience.

Participants have often told me that they've remembered the images of their photographs for more than five years. In addition to the visual power of the exercise, the camera, during his periods of sightlessness, will also experience a magnification of his four other senses.

After taking four to six photographs, the camera and the photographer trade places.

Because the experience is so compelling, a beautiful rapport is established between the photographer and the human camera. It's heart-warming to observe grandparents and grandchildren, and other pairings, carefully guide each other and delight in the wondrous scenes of nature around them.

You can experience by yourself how *Camera* intensifies awareness. Select an outdoor site with varied terrain that's mostly clear of obstructions. Since you'll be walking alone, take along a hiking staff or pole for security and guidance.

Choose a safe route leading to interesting features such as large rocks, trees, and, perhaps, an arresting view. Close your eyes and begin walking, feeling the warmth of the sun and the wind blowing against your body. Notice your leg muscles compensating for the unevenness of the terrain, and the insects singing and buzzing nearby.

When you sense that you're near something intriguing, open your eyes to take its picture. (Looking for the suggested three seconds keeps the attention sharply focused on the subject the whole time. The mind tends to wander when the exposures are longer.)

Continue to tread carefully while taking a few more photographs. As you walk, you can (as needed to stay on course) open your eyes just enough to detect blurry shapes.

1. Sensitively guide the camera by holding his hand and gently pulling his arm in the direction you want to go. Go slowly and remain watchful for obstacles on the ground, low-lying tree branches, etc.

2. Make the photographs stunning by taking shots from unusual angles and perspectives. For example, you can both lie down under a tree and take your picture looking upward, or you can put your camera very close to a tree's bark or leaves.

3. You can prepare the camera for the next picture by telling him which lens to use. For a picture of a flower, tell the camera to choose a close-up lens; for a sweeping scenic panorama, a wide-angle lens; and for a far-away object, a telephoto lens. Such specific instructions help the camera focus on the intended subject when it may not otherwise be obvious.

4. Photographers can also pan the camera—i.e., move it slowly with the shutter held open, like a movie camera. While panning, you can keep the shutter open longer, since the movement will hold the camera's interest. You can also pan vertically—for example, start at the base of a tree and slowly move up the trunk to the highest branches.

5. After you and your partner have played both roles, each of you can sketch from memory one of the pictures he took while playing the role of camera. Then have each camera give his developed picture to the photographer he partnered with.

SILENT SHARING WALK

n *Silent Sharing Walks* participants stroll serenely through beautiful natural areas. In groups of two or three, they walk slowly and silently, communing with nature's wonders. The harmony they experience during this exercise opens their hearts to all creation.

One evening at dusk, in a mountain forest in Southern California, twelve teenage boys and I experienced a magical *Silent Sharing Walk*. We walked slowly down a forest track that overlooked the great Mojave Desert. The electrified silence vibrated with insect and bird song. When a walker saw something captivating, he tapped the shoulder of the nearest boy, and pointed to whatever he had noticed.

We spotted a doe, calmly browsing our way. When we arrived within thirty feet of the deer, she raised her head and serenely gazed at us. Her innocent, trusting manner touched us deeply—we felt completely accepted by this gentle forest native.

Later, three coyotes came trotting toward us. They were as curious as puppies, coming closer a few feet, stopping and howling as they tipped their heads from side to side watching us, wondering what were these silent strangers.

During *Silent Sharing Walks*, animals feel our state of mind and our peaceful, harmonious intent. In silence, we feel a common bond with the rest of life and sense the One that flows through all.

Even during short, mid-day *Silent Sharing Walks*, players can enter, for a time, a magical and loving world.

∾ *To practice* ∾
SILENT SHARING WALK

The ideal number for a *Silent Sharing Walk* is two or three walkers. If the group is larger, divide into sharing teams of two or three people.

Tell the participants to walk in silence. When one walker sees something captivating, instead of speaking aloud about it, he or she should gently tap the shoulder of one or more teammates, then point to the object and silently share the enjoyment.

Choose an attractive trail or open area that's easy to wander through. Since sharing teams move slowly, the distance they travel won't be great. If there are several sharing teams, agree on a time and place to gather afterwards.

Silent Sharing Walkers experience a beautiful rapport among themselves and with nature. Keeping silent and sharing non-verbally, the walkers become fully present with nature and with one another. It's moving to observe the serene, childlike love of the walkers as they gather around newly discovered flora, bird nests, and other natural wonders.

The TRAIL of BEAUTY

"The hours when the mind is
absorbed by beauty are the only hours
when we really live."

—*Richard Jefferies*

his meditation walk is one of the most enjoyable and easily practiced exercises in this book. During this activity, players walk a beautiful trail and read uplifting quotations that inspire feelings of communion with the surrounding landscape.

I tell participants, "As you walk, read and reflect on the quotations and feel the inspiration from the natural beauty around you. You'll find that each quotation encourages loving interaction and oneness with the natural world. Some quotations are accompanied by exercises. The purpose of these exercises is to give you your own experience of nature."

This meditation walk helps people see with new eyes. In the Scottish Highlands I once set up a *Trail of Beauty* along a path that eventually arrived at the front door of a nature center. After completing the exercise, the center's director exclaimed, "Every day for twenty years I've walked this path, but it wasn't until today that I have really *seen* it."

In 1991, two years after the Berlin Wall was torn down, I visited the former East Germany to give Sharing Nature workshops.

According to a 2012 University of Chicago study, 72 percent of east Germans have never believed in the existence of a Creator. During one workshop, my West German translators accompanied the former East German participants as they read *Trail of Beauty* quotations, such as this one by John Muir:

> O these vast, calm, measureless mountain days,
> days in whose light everything seems equally divine, opening a thousand windows to show us God.

The east Germans reflected on the quotations, gazed at the vibrant landscape, and practiced the exercises. Afterwards, several east Germans told my translators that this was the first time they had felt a tangible spiritual presence permeating all life.

Reading how luminaries such as Thoreau, Lao Tzu, Helen Keller, and Richard Jefferies experienced nature uplifts our own experience.

It's easy to share *The Trail of Beauty* exercise with a few friends. Begin by finding a trail or an area that has close, intimate views as well as expansive ones. Place the 8½ x 11 inch quotation signs at locations where the words and the surrounding environment complement each other.

Find the Best Place is a variation of *The Trail of Beauty* that works especially well with young children. In this version, give each child a quotation and have the child draw a picture on it. Then ask each child to find the best location for his quotation. Create a *Trail of Beauty* connecting all the "best places." Use simple quotations, such as this one by John Muir:

> Happy is the man to whom
> every tree is a friend.

You can download and print twelve quotation signs and have your own experience of *The Trail of Beauty* exercise by going to www.sky-earth.org. If you laminate them, you'll be able to use the quotation signs on rainy and windy days. Bring along clothespins so that you can place the signs wherever you wish.

The Trail of Beauty for Groups:

This exercise works well with large groups too. The length of trail should be 100 to 150 yards, to give the walkers enough space to spread out, and you enough room to set out up to a dozen quotation signs. Make sure to space the signs so that the walkers have time to reflect on each quotation before they come upon the next one.

Gather all the participants at the beginning of the trail, and tell them that they will walk the trail one at a time—in silence—so that each walker can feel alone with nature. Encourage them to go at their own pace, and that it's okay to pass someone who is taking more time. If there's a large group, have everyone begin at intervals of 15 seconds or so, and ask them to be conscious as they're walking of the pace of the group. Tell the group it's okay for more than one person at a time to read a sign.

After introducing the exercise, choose someone to stay behind with the group. This person's job will be to signal each of the walkers when to start on the trail. The signaler follows the last walker and collects all the signs and clothespins. This arrangement allows you to go ahead of the group, put up any signs you haven't yet placed, and be at the end of the trail as people finish.

When you have a class of children or a large group of adults, you may want to give each walker something quiet to do or to read while he or she waits for the rest of the group to finish. Or you can ask them to write their own quotations on how nature inspires them.

WRITE YOUR OWN QUOTATION

While outdoors, John Muir saw harmony and unity everywhere. When he gazed at the beautiful symmetry of an island, or the harmonious colors in a flower, he felt that these were visible signs of a divine intelligence. What do *you* feel when you're outdoors? What words would you use to describe your experience of nature?

Write your own quotation telling why it's important to spend quiet time in nature. Express yourself simply and powerfully.

My Nature Quotation:

_____

_____

_____

_____

JOURNEY *to the* HEART *of* NATURE

elen, a participant in one of my Sharing Nature workshops, told me a delightful story from her birding trip to Kenya. While she was standing with a couple of friends at a trail crossing, five Masai tribesmen walked up. Helen wanted to ask them if a certain bird lived nearby, but couldn't speak their language.

She flipped through her bird book and showed the Masai a picture of the bird she wanted to see. The Masai men smiled, began to imitate the bird's behavior, then pointed to where it could be found. The birders, thrilled to have such knowledgeable guides, showed the Masai several more pictures. The Masai mimicked each bird's mannerisms and pointed to its likely whereabouts. Helen was amazed at how well the Masai knew the local birds.

Then, without being shown a picture, the Masai acted out a bird of their own choosing. Now it was the birders' turn to demonstrate their knowledge of African birds. Helen looked through the book until she found the bird she thought the Masai were mimicking. Five delighted smiles told Helen her guess was right.

Native people's intimate knowledge of their environment comes from living close to nature. *Journey to the Heart of Nature* gives us the opportunity to immerse ourselves in a particular natural spot—to listen to the land and enter fully into the lives of its inhabitants.

The exercises below, from the Explorer's Guide for *Journey to the Heart of Nature*, focus and enhance our experience of a natural place.

In this activity, each explorer finds a place outdoors that he especially enjoys. During his visit there (about twenty-five minutes), he chooses a name for his special place and writes it on a card. Later, he will use the card to invite a friend to his area, and he'll also visit his friend's site.

You Are Invited to Explore:

THE GIANT FOREST

Your Guide Is:

JOSEPH

Knowing that they'll later be entertaining a guest and sharing their discoveries, explorers give the *Journey to the Heart of Na-*

ture experience their full attention. Sharing special places is a highlight for the explorers, and a marvelous way for people to connect with one another.

Select a safe area with a variety of natural habitats. Tell your friends where to search for a special place, and make arrangements for everyone to return at the same time. If you are guiding younger children, or adults unfamiliar with the outdoors, use an area with a natural border so that you can keep everyone in view.

Pass out Explorer Guides, pencils, writing boards, and invitation cards. Briefly explain the activities in the Guides and then ask each person to find his own area. When the allotted time has passed, call everyone back.

TO SHARE PLACES:

Have half your friends put their invitation cards into your hat; then have those who still have a card—pick a card out of the hat. The players who draw cards pair up with the owners of their cards. Let's say that Sally draws George's card: Sally keeps his card and gives George her card. By exchanging cards, Sally and George have invited each other to their special places. Give pairs fifteen to twenty minutes to share both their places and exercises they have practiced with one another.

Then assemble everyone and go over the exercises one by one; allow participants to share with the rest of the group their place names, drawings, Vertical Poems, and whatever has inspired them.

EXPLORER'S GUIDE*

Since you won't have time to do every exercise, choose the ones that are most interesting to you and that give you the greatest sense of involvement with your special place.

First Impressions

After choosing a Special Place, take the time to wander around to see what's there. Then pick a spot where you can think about your site, make yourself comfortable, and answer these questions:

1. What are the first things I notice about my site?
2. What do I like about being here?

What Do You Hear?

Listen to the symphony of sounds around you. Concentrate on the distant sounds, and then gradually shift your attention to nearby sounds.

Can you hear the trees singing with the wind? See if you can pick out the song one tree is singing and describe it.

Invitation Card

Choose a name for this special place.

The Name of My Site Is: _____

---

* An attractive handout of this exercise is available at www.sky-earth.org.

Fill out the invitation card with your name and the name of your site.

Sketch Your Best View

Find your favorite view and then draw it. You'll show your drawing to your guest, who will then try to find the view.

More Choices

Practice an exercise from this book such as *Watching the Breath, Nature and Me, Expanding Circles, The Sky and Earth Touched Me,* or *Forest Bathing.*

Share something that makes you smile inside.

Write a Vertical Poem

(See the next chapter for this popular exercise.)

VERTICAL POEM

Because of its contemplative and sharing component, *Vertical Poem* is an excellent bonding activity. To practice this exercise, first observe something that captivates you—perhaps a field of flowers or a secluded sea cove. Notice its effect on you, and choose a word that captures your feeling. Then use each letter of the word to begin a line of your poem.

The simple structure for a vertical poem makes it very easy to write. After successfully crafting their verses, people have exclaimed to me, "It's been forty years since I've written a poem!"

In Taiwan I once led eighty people down a steep, narrow track to a stunning gorge. The trail and chasm were so confining that I couldn't gather the group together. *Vertical Poem* was the perfect exercise for the setting. In the depths of the gorge, eighty people immersed in the chasm scenery, composed their vertical poems. After climbing out of the canyon, many participants read their poems to the group—each poem beautifully expressing our shared experience of the gorge.

Composing a vertical poem quiets a small party of friends and allows them to become more present and immersed in their surroundings.

The *Vertical Poem* below was written in a forest in Northern California:

Fragrances of oak and pine
Open up the heart and mind.
Remain still awhile and listen:
Everywhere is Nature's song—
Sometimes as silent as a leaf falling;
Time is suspended.

—*Tom W.*

To practice
VERTICAL POEM

Write the word you've chosen, one letter on each line. Then use each letter to begin a line of your poem.

___ ______________________________

___ ______________________________

___ ______________________________

___ ______________________________

___ ______________________________

___ ______________________________

___ ______________________________

___ ______________________________

___ ______________________________

The BIRDS
of the AIR

ecause it brings people together to celebrate their oneness with all living things, *The Birds of the Air* song is a marvelous way to conclude a nature outing. The song's beautiful melody and lyrics are accompanied by simple, graceful movements uniting body, mind, and heart.

Once during a lecture at Taipei City Hall, I led four hundred Taiwanese in *The Birds of the Air*. When the Taiwanese began making the song's motions with flowing, Tai Chi-inspired movements, the exquisite interplay of music and grace overwhelmed me.

This exercise awakens and amplifies people's love for the earth and thereby fosters a feeling of stewardship. By expressing gratitude to nature, we invite her reciprocal response. Many times birds have responded to friends singing *The Birds of the Air* by flying to the nearby trees and singing exuberantly.

To share this exercise, go to a place where natural beauty stimulates your friends' higher feelings. Form a half circle with your friends facing a pleasing direction. Stand in front of the group, and repeat the words to the song while you demonstrate the arm motions. As you say each line or phrase, feel its meaning and project those feelings out to your surroundings. For example, while saying, "The trees are my friends," feel your closeness with the trees.

Here are *The Birds of the Air* words (in bold) and accompanying arm motions:

Tell everyone to concentrate on sending to nature thoughts of love and goodwill. Then sing or play *The Birds of the Air* song, inviting everyone to join in. (You can watch a video demonstration of *The Birds of the Air* at www.sky-earth.org. The song is available on this website and also on the Sharing Nature Audio Resources CD; the musical score is in the appendix.)

The BIRDS of the AIR

The birds of the air are my brothers,
Stretch the arms out to the side, turning the palms down.
Gracefully wave the arms as if they were bird wings.

All flowers, my sisters,
Bring the palms together in front of you,
then spread your fingers apart like a flower opening.

The trees are my friends.
Join the palms together above your head
and sway your body like the trunk of a tree.

All living creatures,
Stretch your arms out to the sides in welcome to all creatures.

Mountains,
Bring your fingertips together at chin level to form a mountain peak.

And streams,
Keeping your left hand at the chin, sweep your right arm
out to the side, fluttering the fingers like rippling water.

I take unto my care.
Cup one hand on top of the other, palms up, at heart level,
holding all nature in your care.

For this green earth is our Mother,
Sweep your hands up and out from the heart,
reaching out to include the whole earth.

Hidden in the sky is the Spirit above.
Look upward, extending your arms toward the sky.

I share one Life with all who are here;
Cross your hands at the heart.

To everyone I give my love,
Keep the right hand at your heart, and sweep
the left hand out to the side with the palm up.

To everyone I give my love.
Keep the left hand out to the side, and sweep
the right hand out to the other side, with palm up.

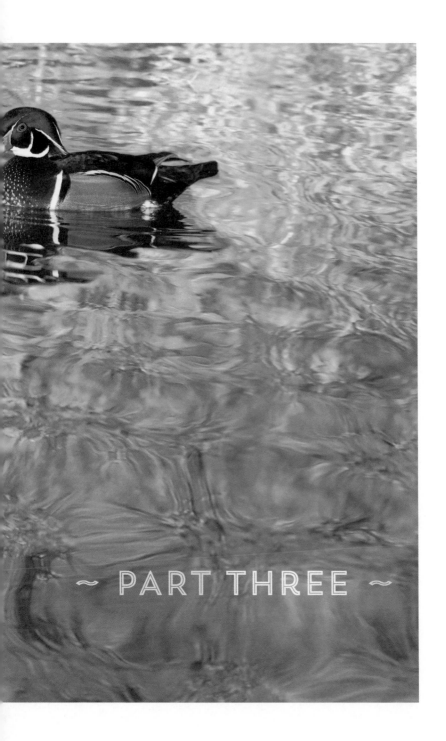

~ PART THREE ~

COMMUNING
with LIFE

"When exposed to
the rays of mountain beauty
[one] glows with joy."

—*John Muir*

o convey nature's spirit to others, we need to experience
nature deeply ourselves. When we visit wild places we feel
a sense of awe and timelessness; nature's purity expands our
awareness so that we touch the wholeness within ourselves.

Richard St. Barbe Baker, forester and earth healer, had an experience in an English wood that set the course for his life. At the
age of five, after much coaxing, St. Barbe convinced his nurse to
let him take his first walk alone in the English woods:

> [A]t first I kept to a path which wound its way down
> into the valley; but soon I found myself in a dense
> part of the forest where the trees were taller and the
> path became lost in bracken beneath the pines. . . . I
> became intoxicated with the beauty [all] around me,
> immersed in the joyousness and exultation of feeling part of it all. . . . The overpowering beauty of it
> all entered my very being. At that moment my heart
> brimmed over with a sense of unspeakable thankfulness which has followed me through the years since
> that woodland re-birth.*

*Richard St. Barbe Baker, *My Life, My Trees* (London: Lutterworth Press, 1970), 10–11.

St. Barbe's passion for trees led him to Kenya in 1920 to begin his social forestry work: to encourage local people to reforest their land. Through his international organization, Men of the Trees, and other organizations he assisted, St. Barbe was responsible for planting twenty-six trillion trees. Wherever St. Barbe traveled, people would suddenly decide to plant a few million trees. His rapport with nature enabled him to inspire countless thousands to re-green the earth.

My own outlook on life changed radically because of my Chico Creek experience of joyous harmony with nature. That day, as I spontaneously felt my consciousness uplifted, the world I saw—overarching trees, flowering shrubs, and vivid blue sky—appeared to me already perfect. I felt clearly that the world didn't need changing—*I* needed changing. I realized that the more deeply I touched life, the more I could share with others. I passionately wanted others to know nature as I had experienced it that day.

SILENCE
CONNECTS US

Our minds are like the switch on a short-wave radio: when the switch is set to "broadcast," all we hear is our own voice talking. We can't *hear* anything else until the switch is turned to "receive."

In the same way, a busy, chattering mind is always in "sending mode." The noise of our own minds prevents us from deeply experiencing and learning from the world around us.

When you are in nature, let your mind stop planning, analyzing, and evaluating. Let it simply witness and appreciate what your senses bring to its attention.

Henry David Thoreau would often sit for hours absorbed in the natural world: "I sat in my sunny doorway from sunrise to noon, rapt in a reverie, amidst the pines and hickories and sumacs, in undisturbed solitude and stillness." These periods of

A replica of Henry David Thoreau's cabin at Walden Pond

stillness, he said, did not "subtract from my life," but added to it, giving him "so much over and above [my] usual allowance."

In *Walden*, Thoreau spoke of passing through an invisible boundary where "universal . . . laws . . . begin to establish themselves around and within" him. In simplicity and stillness, he grew closer to all living things and to Life's higher truths.

TWO WAYS OF SEEING THE WORLD

The cultural historian Richard Tarnas has described two different ways of seeing the world.* In what he describes as the "Modern Worldview," only human beings have intelligence and a soul; everything in the nonhuman world does not. In this view of life, the human self separates itself from the rest of creation.

In Tarnas' description of the "Primal Worldview," consciousness and intelligence pervade all life. Everything

Modern Worldview

* Richard Tarnas, *Cosmos and Psyche* (New York: Viking, 2006), 80.

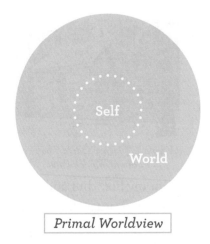

Primal Worldview

has a soul and is animated by a unifying life force. The permeable human self experiences spiritual kinship with all existence.

A French West African tribesman expressed the integration of the "Primal Worldview" in this way: "Deeply felt silences [are] the core of our Kofon religion. During these times, the nature within ourselves [finds] unity . . . in the common nature which pervades all life."

"To ancient thinkers, soul was the mysterious force that gave life and breath to the myriad of the earth's creatures. . . . Later, theologians restricted the possession of a soul to human beings." (Gary A. Kowalksi)

The belief that only humans are conscious and that everything else is dead—or at most dimly conscious, has justified mankind's abuse of his greater environment.

The Sky and Earth Touched Me exercises expand the human self and move us from individual to universal consciousness. The exercises are intuitive and calming, and give us a broader view of life.

Abraham Maslow described peak experiences as accompanied by "feelings of intense happiness and well-being," feelings which often involve "an awareness of transcendental unity." We can encourage such peak experiences by using techniques that focus our complete attention on nature. By regular practice we can turn isolated peak experiences into high plateaus of constant inspiration.

MAKE YOUR IDEALISM
PRACTICAL

In the early 1980s, I created *Flow Learning*, a teaching strategy designed to help people receive the most from their time outdoors. Flow Learning allows us to meet others where they are, and then to guide them sensitively step-by-step toward increasingly profound nature experiences.

Flow Learning is based on learning through deepening and expanding awareness. It provides a simple, natural framework that sequences nature exercises for most profound effect. There are many Sharing Nature exercises for each of the four stages of Flow Learning:

1. Awaken Enthusiasm
2. Focus Attention
3. Experience Directly
4. Share Inspiration

A Flow Learning experience compares to ascending a tall ladder. Just as climbing a ladder gives one greater perspective, so the higher stages of Flow Learning give a more expansive outlook on life.

In the early 1990s, on the German-Polish border, I once gave a three-hour workshop for a lively and diverse group: forty German teenagers, twenty-five German educators, and seventeen mentally challenged Scottish teenagers. Because the program was in the former East Germany, few of the Germans spoke English; none of the Scots spoke German.

I began the session with playful Sharing Nature games to awaken the participants' enthusiasm and to make learning dynamic and fun. Because the games were experiential, everyone could play. It was heartwarming to observe small groups of Germans and Scots communicating with one another despite differences in language, age, and intellectual ability. Flow Learning's first stage, *Awaken Enthusiasm*, established a beautiful rapport and family feeling in the group.

For Flow Learning's second stage, *Focus Attention*, we played calming activities to increase sensory awareness and receptivity. Then I introduced the *Journey to the Heart of Nature* exercise for the *Experience Directly* phase of Flow Learning.

While looking for her special place, one Scottish lass fell into the small river. Once she was safely back on dry land and the excitement was over, the participants sat quietly in their areas absorbed in nature and in the exercise. The Scots and Germans were so focused that I felt like we were in a group meditation. The *Share Inspiration* time became especially heartwarming because of the group's rapport with nature and with one another.

 Readers can learn more about Flow Learning and other nature activities at **www.sharingnature.com** and in the author's book *Sharing Nature: Nature Awareness Activities for All Ages.*

A GIFT OF WHOLENESS

A friend once led a group from New Delhi on a *Sky and Earth Touched Me* walk. These were middle-aged city dwellers who had rarely, if ever, been in the countryside. It was John's first time leading the exercises. Afterwards he spoke to me earnestly:

I was amazed at how easy and fun it was to lead the exercises, and how they took people deeper and deeper. All the participants had tears in their eyes, and they wrote the most beautiful things. Many people told me the walk had changed their life.

Imagine being able to give another person the gift of joy, serenity, and feeling of oneness. People from around the world have shared John's experience leading the exercises. If the wellness exercises in this book have inspired you, I hope you will share them with friends and loved ones.

~ ~ ~

"If you wish your [friends] to think deep thoughts, to know the holiest emotions, take them to the woods and hills, and give them the freedom of the meadows; the hills purify those who walk upon them." —*Richard Jefferies*

LIVING *in* ONENESS

atie—a friend and fellow member of Ananda Village, my home community—shared a beautiful experience with me. One of our gardeners introduced her to a mature oak inhabiting Ananda's Meditation Retreat. The caretaker called the elderly tree Grandfather.

"A few days later," Katie told me, "I was walking past Grandfather Tree when I sensed him calling me. I went over to Grandfather, sat down, and leaned against his trunk. At first, it seemed strange to try to communicate with a tree, but once I stopped thinking, I knew what to do. After a few minutes, I felt a protective, fatherly feeling coming from the tree. I thanked the tree and sent him loving energy in return. When I left the Grandfather Tree, I felt I was welcome to visit him whenever I needed.

"On a subsequent visit, I asked the Grandfather Tree, 'How do *you* experience God?'

"At first, my own thoughts answered for him; but after these thoughts quieted down, I *felt* his answer:

Love.

"Warm, gentle love emanated from Grandfather Tree into my body—I was able to experience the way that *he* experienced love.

"Then Grandfather spoke in my heart:

All of nature is love. Everything is love. And it is all One. I experience this love continuously.

"From Grandfather I understood that all nature—the flowers, the trees, the rivers—want to share in this love with us. The flowers want us to stop for a moment and give them our loving touch. The trees want us to stop and share in a moment of still-ness. They want to smile at us and for us to smile back, but we never stop to look upon their shining faces.

'We must open our hearts and eyes to see the gifts of life around us. If we do,' Grandfather said, **'We will be able to remember our oneness.'"**

Katie told me that now, wherever she goes, she feels a wondrous love and rapport with nature. "Love one another," Katie says, "means to love not only the human race, but all existence."

The Sky and Earth Touched Me
ONLINE RESOURCES

Whether you desire to deepen your experience of nature or to share with friends, the *Online Resources* page makes it easy to download and print exercise handouts and additional instructional aids. For a nominal fee you can access

- ✽ printable PDF handouts for ten wellness exercises,

- ✽ twelve Trail of Beauty signs,

- ✽ mp3 and video of *The Birds of the Air* song and arm movements, and

- ✽ instructional videos by Joseph Cornell on *The Sky and Earth Touched Me* exercises and program.

WWW.SKY-EARTH.ORG

Sharing Nature®
WORLDWIDE

THE NATURE AWARENESS WORK
of Joseph Bharat Cornell

oseph Bharat Cornell is the founder and president of Sharing Nature Worldwide, one of the planet's most widely respected nature awareness programs. He is the honorary president of Japan Sharing Nature Association, which has 224 regional associations and 10,000 members.

He is the author of the Sharing Nature Book Series, used by millions of parents, educators, naturalists, and youth and religious leaders all over the world. Mr. Cornell's second book, *Listening to Nature*, has inspired thousands of adults to deepen their relationship with nature.

The U.S. Fish & Wildlife Service selected his first book, *Sharing Nature with Children*, as one of the 15 most influential books published since 1890 for connecting children to nature.

Cornell's highly effective outdoor learning strategy, Flow Learning™, was featured by the U.S. National Park Service as one of five recommended learning theories, along with the work of Maria Montessori, Howard Gardner, John Dewey, and Jean Piaget.

Mr. Cornell has received many international awards for his Sharing Nature books and work. He has received the prestigious Countess Sonja-Bernadotte Prize in Germany for his vast influence on environmental education in Central Europe. In 2011 Cornell was selected as one of the "100 biggest opinion leaders committed to the Environment" by the French organization, Anges Gardiens de la Planète.

Known for his warmth and joyful enthusiasm, Cornell "has a genius for finding the essence of a subject, explaining it in clear and compelling ways, and then giving the reader creative exercises to gain an actual experience."

Joseph and his wife, Anandi, are senior ministers and residents of Ananda Village, in Northern California.

For more information about Joseph Cornell's books and activities visit: **www.jcornell.org**

SHARING NATURE
WELLNESS PROGRAM

 ohn Muir said, "Nature's peace flows into us as sunshine flows into trees." Nature, the great Healer, offers gifts of joyful serenity and vitality to every receptive heart.

During a Sharing Nature Wellness program you'll practice nature meditation exercises to quiet your mind, expand your consciousness, and open your heart to all creation. You will learn how to internalize your experience of nature and feel more at peace with life.

You'll delight in joyful nature awareness activities, feel more positive and affirmative, and feel a spirit of community and communion with others and with nature.

Nature's benevolent presence will remind you of life's higher priorities.

Sharing Nature Wellness programs provide uplifting experiences and healing through nature for individuals, and for leaders in business, education, religion, and the public sector. Courses can include instruction in meditation if desired.

To sponsor a program or find out more about Sharing Nature please visit **www.sharingnature.com**, or contact us at this address:

Sharing Nature Worldwide

14618 Tyler Foote Road box   Phone: (530) 478-7650
Nevada City, CA 95959   Email: info@sharingnature.com

APPENDIX

THE BIRDS OF THE AIR

words by Joseph Cornell, *music by* Michael Starner-Simpson

The birds of the air are my bro - thers, All flow-ers my sis-ters, the

trees are my friends. All liv-ing crea- tures, mountains and streams,

I take un - to my care. For this green earth is our mo - ther,

hid-den in the sky is the spi - rit a - bove.

I share one life wi - ith all who are here; to ev-ry-one I give my

love, to ev - ry - one I give my love.

PHOTOGRAPHIC
and
GRAPHIC CREDITS

This book features photographs and images from a number of photographers and artists, printed or reprinted with their kind permission. To each one, the author extends his heartfelt appreciation.

5. © Sharing Nature Worldwide Photographs (Greg Sundara Traymar)
7. Tamarack Song: © Eric Valli
10. © Alessandro Rovelli
12–13. © Heart of Nature Photography (Robert Frutos)
14. © Heart of Nature Photography (Robert Frutos)
17. © John Hendrickson Photography
18. © John Hendrickson Photography
22. © Joyful Photography (Barbara Bingham)
24. Two aspens—both: © John Hendrickson Photography
25. © John Hendrickson Photography
26. © Hansa Trust (J. Donald Walters)
28. © Alessandro Rovelli
30. © Joyful Photography (Barbara Bingham)
31. © Ananda Archives
32. © John Hendrickson Photography
34. © Heart of Nature Photography (Robert Frutos)
36. © Heart of Nature Photography (Robert Frutos)
38. © Heart of Nature Photography (Robert Frutos)
40. © Alessandro Rovelli
44. © KentWilliamsPhotography.com
46. © Heart of Nature Photography (Robert Frutos)
47. © Giorgio Majno
49. © John Hendrickson Photography
50. © Heart of Nature Photography (Robert Frutos)
52. © Joyful Photography (Barbara Bingham)
53. © KentWilliamsPhotography.com

MORE INSPIRATION
from Joseph Bharat Cornell

Listening to Nature
How to Deepen Your Awareness of Nature

The beloved and bestselling book *Listening to Nature* will open your eyes and your heart to the peace and joyous spirit of the natural world.

Joseph Bharat Cornell offers adults a sensitive and lively guide to deeper awareness of nature. Cornell's innovative nature awareness techniques combine with stunning photographs and quotations from famous naturalists to enliven your experience of nature. This new edition has been extensively rewritten and includes dozens of new photographs and quotations.

"A splendid masterpiece that captures the 'Oneness' we are all seeking to achieve with Nature" —**Tom Brown, Jr.**, Founder of Living Tree Educational Foundation, author of *The Tracker*

Sharing Nature
Nature Awareness Activities for All Ages

Sharing Nature with Children, selling more than half a million copies, sparked a worldwide revolution in nature education. Now that classic has been rewritten—with new activities and games—and combined with *Sharing Nature with Children II*, in one complete volume. This new version of a beloved nature handbook and phenomenal teaching tool incorporates the author's latest insights.

AUM: The Melody of Love

AUM is God's tangible presence in creation. By hearing the Cosmic Sound, conscious contact with Spirit is established. Saint Francis described celestial AUM as "music so sweet and beautiful that, had it lasted a moment longer, I would have melted away from the sheer joy of it."

AUM is vibrating blissfully in every atom in the universe; when one listens to it, he enters into the stream of God's love. Communion with AUM expands one's consciousness and unites him with Spirit.

"Cornell invites us, through AUM, into the very source of nature, the fount of universal religious experience, and the essential experience of self. This intriguing book could very well change the way you see everything."
    —**Garth Gilchrist**, nature writer, storyteller, portrayer of John Muir

Crystal Clarity Publishers offers a great number of additional resources to assist you on your life journey, including many other books, and a wide variety of inspirational and relaxation music and videos. To find out more information, please contact us at:

www.crystalclarity.com
14618 Tyler Foote Road / Nevada City, CA 95959
TOLL FREE 800.424.1055 or 530.478.7600
FAX: 530.478.7610
EMAIL: clarity@crystalclarity.com